Draw Mandala Doodles

CREATE BEAUTIFUL DESIGNS THAT UNLOCK CREATIVITY AND INSPIRE RELAXATION AND FOCUS

Carolyn Scrace

STERLING INNOVATION
New York

STERLING INNOVATION
New York

An Imprint of Sterling Publishing
387 Park Avenue South
New York, NY 10016

© 2015 by Salariya Book Company Ltd
Illustrations © 2015 Salariya Book Company Ltd

ISBN 978-1-4351-5250-2

This book is part of the *Draw Mandala Doodles* kit
and is not to be sold separately.

For information about custom editions,
special sales, and premium and
corporate purchases, please contact
Sterling Special Sales at 800-805-5489
or specialsales@sterlingpublishing.com.

Manufactured in China

2 4 6 8 10 9 7 5 3 1

www.sterlingpublishing.com

Contents

Chapter One

Mandala Doodle Basics

Doodling is a wonderful way to unwind and have fun. It can boost artistic confidence, and provides the perfect opportunity for developing creativity. The repetitive nature of doodling simultaneously focuses the mind while producing a sense of inner calm, tranquility, and emotional well-being.

Meditation

Both doodling and mandalas are powerful tools used in meditation. The act of doodling a mandala can help focus your consciousness.

Explore

This book is designed to enable you to get the maximum enjoyment and relaxation from doodling. Learn about color theory and the different tools and materials to use. Explore basic coloring and shading techniques with simple, step-by-step instructions to guide you. Find out how to construct and design mandalas and how to use themes in your patterns.

Each chapter finishes with a design outline to inspire you. It's ready for you to adapt, doodle, and embellish however you wish!

Mandalas & meditation

Origins...

"Mandala" is a Sanskrit word meaning "circle". The earliest mandala designs date from the fourth century, originating in Tibet, India, Nepal, Japan, Bhutan, China, and Indonesia.

Spiritual guide

In Hinduism and Buddhism the mandala is a symbolic, geometric diagram that represents the universe. The mandala is used in meditation, as a focus for universal forces. By mentally entering the mandala and moving toward its center, one is spiritually guided through the processes of disintegration and integration. Disintegration reflects mankind's increasing alienation from nature, while integration symbolizes the level of complete or supreme enlightenment. Depicted in this way, enlightenment is a state of beauty, harmony, and color.

Mandalas painted in sand

In Tibetan art, exquisite mandalas are created from sand. Millions of grains of colored sand are painstakingly laid into place over a period of days or weeks. Traditionally most sand mandalas are destroyed shortly after their completion to symbolize the impermanence of life. The sands are poured into a nearby river or stream so the waters carry healing energies throughout the world.

Sand mandala

Focus of energy

Mandalas are used for meditation, prayer, and healing. The process of meditation can teach our mind and body a new consciousness; using a mandala focuses this energy. It is an effective tool for clearing the mind of clutter and calming the soul. The act of designing, drawing, and doodling a mandala is a powerful spiritual experience and a positive form of art therapy.

Using a mandala to meditate

Place your mandala at eye level in a warm, well-lit spot. You may wish to have objects nearby that you feel will help to quiet your mind.

Sit comfortably, relax, and close your eyes. Breathe deeply, let go of all worry and tension. Visualize the mandala and focus your energy. Carry on breathing deeply until you are ready to open your eyes.

Look at the center of your mandala with your eyes slightly out of focus. Keep your eyes on the center, but at the same time allow your vision to see other elements of the design.

Now focus your eyes, slowly journey through the mandala from the outside toward the center. Experience the flow of energy and feel the harmony of balance and wholeness within.

Fill in background areas using a thick-tipped **marker pen**. Fine-tipped, permanent marker pens are ideal for outlines and detail.

Marker pens

Colored ink splats and washes produce exciting backgrounds for doodles. Paint areas of your design with diluted colored ink. When dry, doodle over the luminous colors.

Colored inks

Tools & materials

There really are no special tools and materials needed to doodle a mandala. Some of the most effective doodled mandalas have been done using an old pencil stub on a scrap of paper and drawing around a cup and some coins. However, to fully enjoy the experience of doodling you may wish to use some or all of the tools and materials suggested here. Experiment with different combinations of techniques and other types of materials. Use whatever inspires you creatively!

Felt-tip pens

Felt-tip pens come in a range of thicknesses. Thick pens are ideal for blocking in large areas of color.

Gel pens

Gel pens produce a flowing line. White and metallic gel pens are ideal for doodling onto colored paper and on top of dark-colored doodles.

Ruler

Protractor

Fine-liner pens

Fine-liner pens come in a vast range of colors. They are perfect for coloring in small areas. Use fine-liner pens for adding delicate doodled patterns.

Bristol board

Use smooth **Bristol board** to work on with pencils, pencil crayons, markers, felt-tips, gel, and fine-liner pens for adding fine detail.

Drawing paper

Drawing paper comes in a variety of weights. Heavyweight paper is good for painting washes. Note: ink lines can bleed on some cartridge paper.

Graphite pencils

Graphite pencils come in different grades, from hard to soft. Use a medium pencil for roughs and thumbnails. Try slightly harder pencils for drawing out your design. Soft pencils are ideal for adding areas of shading.

Pencil crayons

Pencil crayons are ideal for softly shading an area. Use them for coloring in. Try layering different colors to create depth and add texture.

Getting started

The quickest and easiest way to draw a circular mandala is to use a selection of templates to trace around: plates, cups, coins, or lids.

Hold your plate or saucer firmly down on the paper, and draw around it in pencil. Next, use a ruler to draw horizontal and vertical guidelines through the center.

Start drawing in smaller circles from the center outward. Use the guidelines to help position the templates when you trace around them.

Keep your initial design simple. Just relax, free your mind, and enjoy doodling!

Note: turn to pages 14-15 to see how to doodle some of these patterns.

Using a protractor

A protractor enables you to divide a circular mandala into any number of equal sections. There are 360 degrees in a circle, so if you want six sections simply divide 360° by 6 = 60°. Then use the protractor to mark out increments of 60°, eg. 60°, 120°, 180°, 240°. Note: there are two sets of numbers on a protractor, one running from left to right and the other from right to left.

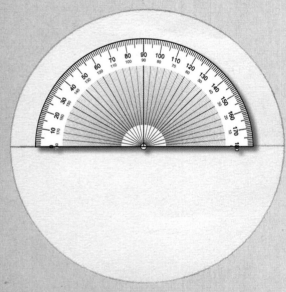

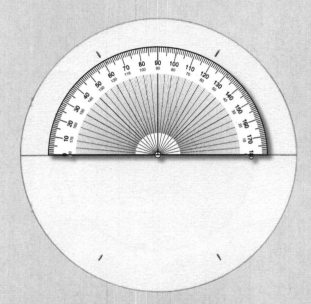

Draw a circle, then add a horizontal line through the center. Place the protractor on the line, aligning it with the center.

Mark out the size (in degrees) of each section. Draw in a line from the center through each mark to the outside edge.

To make 12 sections, divide 360° by 12 = 30°. Mark out 30° sections until the circle is complete.

Pattern building

Start...

Doodling patterns is easy! Start by drawing a series of simple lines. Add a circle, then put dots around the outside. Draw a spiral in the center and triangles around the outside...

...draw heart shapes, add stripes, curls...

Relax...

Relax, free your mind, don't think of what you are drawing—let your creativity take over. Every mark you make on the paper comes from your innate artistic talent. Embrace the liberating experience of doodling.

...let the patterns evolve, slightly changing the shape of the design each time you draw. Add stripes, spots, or dots...

This simple mandala has been doodled using some of the patterns just created.

Deconstructing
Line, shape, and color

An artist achieves a pattern through the use of lines, shapes, and colors. If you have a complicated pattern you wish to doodle, break it down into these simple components. Think of drawing patterns as line weaving, creating shapes and using color to give them substance.

For this woven pattern, start by drawing a pencil grid:

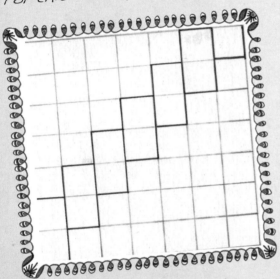

Draw in rectangles running diagonally (as above).

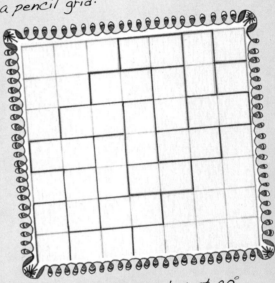

Add more rectangles at 90° to the first set.

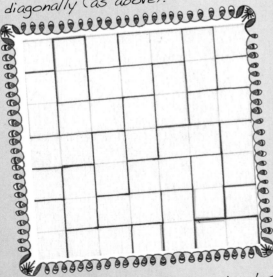

Repeat the rows of rectangles at alternating angles.

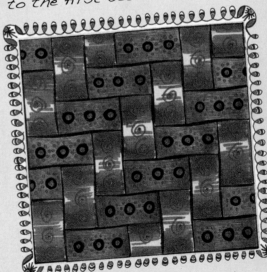

Use felt-tip and gel pens to color in and doodle the pattern.

14

To doodle this geometric pattern, start by drawing a pencil grid:

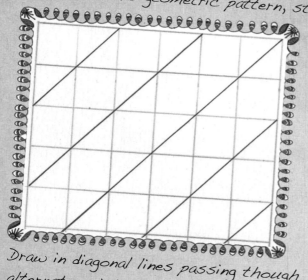

Draw in diagonal lines passing though alternate points.

Add diagonal lines at 90° to the first set.

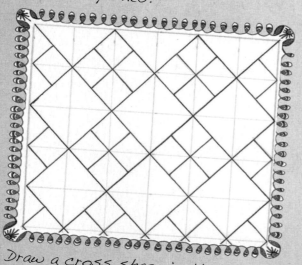

Draw a cross shape in the center of alternate boxes.

Now draw a smaller square shape inside each blank box.

Add cross shapes to each small square and diagonal cross shapes inside the large squares.

Use felt-tip and gel pens to color in and doodle the pattern.

15

Color theory

Primary colors

To an artist the primary colors (red, yellow, and blue) are the three colors of pigment that cannot be mixed from any other colors. All other colors are derived from these three primaries.

Secondary colors

Green, orange, and purple are called secondary colors. They are formed by mixing pairs of primary colors.

Tertiary colors

The six tertiary colors are created by mixing primary and secondary colors. They are red-orange, red-purple, blue-purple, blue-green, yellow-green, and yellow-orange.

Complementary colors

Colors that lie opposite on the color diagram (page 17) are complementary colors. For example, red and green clash when used together, creating vibrant color schemes.

Analogous colors

Colors that lie adjacent to each other on the color diagram are analogous colors. They produce harmonious color schemes, for example blue and purple, red and orange.

Red

Purple

Orange

Blue

Yellow

Green

Red-purple

Red-orange

Blue-purple

Yellow-orange

Blue-green

Yellow-green

Colorful emotions!

Color can dramatically affect feelings and emotions. Red, orange, and yellow are known as warm colors. They evoke emotions ranging from feelings of comfort and love to those of anger and hostility. Blue, purple, and green are referred to as cold colors and reflect peace and tranquility. They can also evoke feelings of sadness or grief.

17

Light & shade

Technique

Adding areas of shading to doodled shapes gives the illusion of depth to the overall design. There are many different techniques that can be used to add tone, for example scribbling, hatching, and crosshatching.

Hatching

Hatching is a series of parallel lines. The closer together the lines are, the darker the shade of tone that is created.

Crosshatching

Crosshatching is like hatching but with a second series of parallel lines that crisscrosses over it. The denser the crosshatching, the darker the tonal value.

Scribbling

Scribbling produces interesting textures. To create dark tones, simply make the scribbles denser.

Practice

Try shading some solid objects such as a cube and a cylinder. Once you have mastered the techniques of shading you can start to apply them to doodles.

First choose the direction of the light (light source). Then add shade to the parts that face away from the light.

Before and after...

The mandala (left) looks flat and uninteresting. However, the addition of shading transforms the design, making it appear three-dimensional and vibrant (below). Shading has been added to part of the border, giving a rich, textured appearance.

Light source

19

Chapter Two
Lotus Mandala

The immaculate lotus flower that emerges each morning from the muddy waters below can be seen as a symbol of both purity and rebirth. As the blossom breaks through the surface of the water it represents spiritual enlightenment.

Sketchbook

Try to keep a small sketchbook or notepad with you at all times to jot down ideas for doodles and mandala designs. Quick sketches make invaluable visual reminders for future doodling.

Snapshots

These sketchbook pages (below) were inspired by a visit to a garden center where some exquisite lotus flowers were on display. If you don't have time to make sketches, take snapshots to work from later.

A fully opened lotus flower represents a person's total self-awareness and enlightenment.

Side view of a lotus flower

A closed lotus flower is symbolic of the time before a person achieves enlightenment.

23

Pencil rough
Composition

All the patterns and drawings from your sketchbook can be brought together to make up the final composition. The overhead view of the lotus blossom makes an ideal focus for the center of the design. Use the side view as a repeat pattern to make a bold border design. The flower buds are perfect for a delicate pattern around the edges.

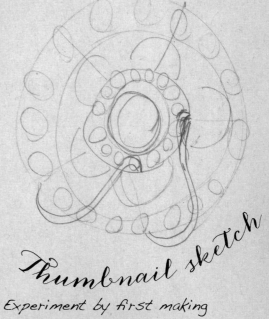

Thumbnail sketch

Experiment by first making a thumbnail sketch of your composition.

Amazingly, not only are most parts of the lotus plant edible, it has also been used in traditional Asian medicine for many centuries!

Lotus roots! Great doodle inspiration...

24

This exciting inner border pattern is derived from lotus roots.

The sinuous stems of the pure lotus blossoms reach out into the murky depths below.

Add shading to your rough— this will help you decide on tonal values for your final mandala artwork.

Color scheme
Meanings of color

In Buddhism the color of a lotus flower has a significant bearing on the symbolism associated with it. A white lotus flower represents purity of spirit and the mind. The pink lotus flower is usually associated with the Buddha. A red lotus flower relates to love, passion, and compassion. The blue lotus flower signifies wisdom and knowledge. A purple lotus flower is symbolic of mysticism and spirituality. Lastly, a gold or yellow lotus flower represents the gaining of enlightenment.

Color rough

It is a good idea to make a color rough before you start on the final artwork. In this case the original design has been quickly colored in to try out this color palette. As with any preparatory roughs and sketches, color roughs are only instinctive guides, they don't have to be adhered to. Your ideas may well change and develop as you doodle the mandala.

Draw out the finished design...

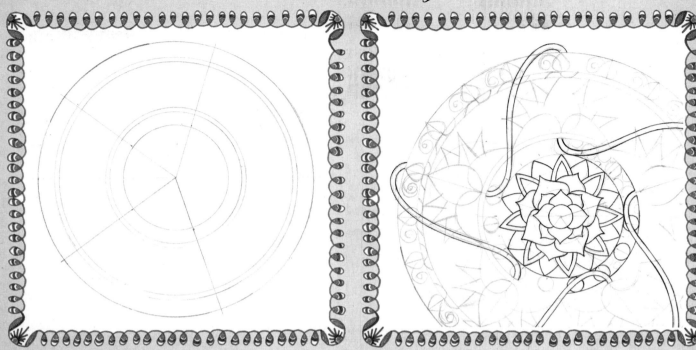

Use a pencil to draw in concentric circles. Divide the mandala into five equal sections by measuring out 72° increments with a protractor.

Draw the main pattern shapes in pencil. Once you are happy with the design, go over the lines in black fine-liner or ball-point pen.

Fill in the main areas of color. Start working from the center outward.

Now relax, have fun, and start doodling into your mandala!

Inspiration...

Use this finished artwork (above) as inspiration for your own lotus mandala. The outline of the design is printed on the opposite page. It is ready for you to adapt, doodle, and embellish however you wish!

29

Chapter Three
Spiral Mandala

Potent symbol

The spiral is a powerful symbol that reflects universal patterns of growth and evolution. It is a very feminine symbol, representing the goddess, fertility, and the cycle of life. The spiral can be a symbol of creation, as well as a potent symbol of disorder and chaos.

Prehistoric rock carvings of spiral shapes are believed by many to be early solar calendars that follow the movement of the sun over the course of the year. The spiral is frequently used as a symbol of life, death, and rebirth; consequently many ancient tombs are embellished with spiral designs.

Asymmetrical designs

Traditional mandalas are symmetrical designs. Although spiral-shaped mandalas evolve from a central point they are not symmetrical about their horizontal and vertical axes, and are therefore described as asymmetrical.

Nature's patterns

The natural world abounds with spiral shapes—for example, the center of a sunflower, the patterned structure of a pinecone, the whorl of a shell, and the path of a hurricane—even some galaxies spiral! Spirals are dynamic and exciting; they make fascinating shapes for creating a powerful doodle design.

Take inspiration from nature—make notes and quick sketches, or take photographs of spiral shapes and patterns that you come across. Doodle any patterns that you see. If you haven't got a sketchbook handy, use any scrap of paper.

A conch shell's spiral shape reflects the celestial movement of the galaxy.

Conch shell

Pinecone pattern

Ancient Mayan
symbolism depicted
wind gods riding
snail shells!

Spiral shell: symbol of
expanding consciousness!

Draw a spiral
Color rough

Use the images from your sketchbook as a starting point to create a rough mandala design. The natural flow of this design lends itself to using the colors of the rainbow, beginning with red and ending with violet.

Using a pencil, draw a circle.
Draw a spiral shape from the
center of the circle outward
to the circumference.

Draw in a horizontal line that
bisects the circle. Using a
protractor, mark out 18 equal
sections in 20° increments.

Add straight lines radiating out from
the center. Using these as a guide,
gradually draw in curvy lines.

Finish the design by drawing in curved
triangular shapes. Ink in the drawing
with black fine-liner or ball-point pen.

Rainbow colors

Watercolor wash

Working outward from the center, use a clean paintbrush and fresh water to wet small sections of the spiral. Start by adding red watercolor. Wash the brush and add a section of orange watercolor. Blend the two colors together before the paint dries. Repeat this process with the other colors of the rainbow. To make your finished artwork look more vibrant, keep the watercolor paint fairly transparent, with areas of white paper showing through.

Having finished all the preparatory work, it's time to really have fun doodling! Once you start doodling your spiral mandala, let go of the mundane, everyday world. Relax your mind, leave worries behind, and let your creativity flow.

Dramatic black

For added dramatic effect fill in the outer shapes with black marker pen.

Analogous colors

Use analogous colors when doodling the mandala. (Turn to pages 16-17 for helpful notes and a color diagram).

You can leave these areas plain black. However, a medium-sized white or metallic silver gel pen is ideal for adding more finishing touches to the design.

Inspiration...

Use this finished artwork (above) as inspiration for your own spiral mandala. The outline of the design is printed on the opposite page. It is ready for you to adapt, doodle, and embellish however you wish!

39

Chapter Four
Love & Passion

Historically the shape of a heart has been recognized as a symbol for love, charity, happiness, and compassion. Use repeating heart-shaped doodles to mirror the rhythmic beat of life within our own bodies and in the world around us.

Pattern weaving

Weave a never-ending pattern of heart shapes to reflect eternal love. Free your mind and think passionately about the people and things that you love.

41

Composition

Celtic influences...

Heart shapes provide the central theme for this mandala, which is further enhanced by doodles inspired by Celtic patterns. Use a strong central design like the four linked heart shapes to create a bold composition. The border design carries on the Celtic theme with entwined hearts. To complete the composition add a broad band of hearts, tilted at an angle to draw attention to the center of the mandala.

Rough sketch of the composition...

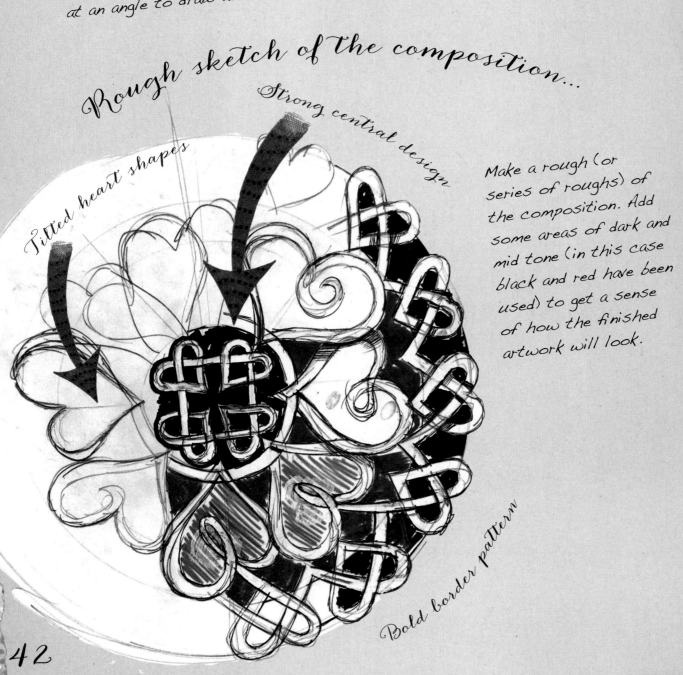

Tilted heart shapes

Strong central design

Bold border pattern

Make a rough (or series of roughs) of the composition. Add some areas of dark and mid tone (in this case black and red have been used) to get a sense of how the finished artwork will look.

Doodles inspired by Celtic patterns

These continuous heart patterns have no beginning and no end, reflecting eternal love...

Roses

Apples

Maple leaves

Turtle doves

Symbols...

Design some meaningful doodle patterns to include in your artwork. The rose, for example, is a symbol of love and romance. Apples symbolize love and fertility, peace and adoration. The maple leaf is a symbol of love and sweetness. Turtle doves symbolize friendship, love, and devotion as well as peace and tranquility.

Lace is associated with love and romance.

43

Shades of red

Ink wash

Creating an exciting background for your mandala can liberate your creativity and add a cohesive quality to your design and color scheme.

It's best to use heavy watercolor or drawing paper. Lightly pencil in the circular shape of the mandala. Use a large, clean paintbrush (or sponge) and fresh water to wet the paper. Load your brush with red ink then paint a swirling circle within the mandala shape. The ink will run and bleed, making exciting patterns to doodle over. Leave until the ink is completely dry.

Pencil in your mandala design. Using a protractor, mark out 22.5° increments to position the 16 heart shapes in the outer border. Ink in the finished design then erase any pencil construction lines.

Experiment!
Try doodling on top of an ink wash...

44

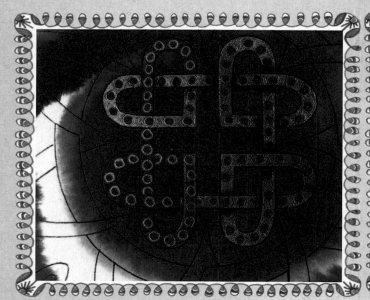

Gold gel pen adds a richness that "lifts" the central design from its dark red background. Use black ball-point hatching to create the effect of the heart shapes weaving over and under.

Doodle some small hearts and use a purple fine-liner to fill in the background to add tonal depth.

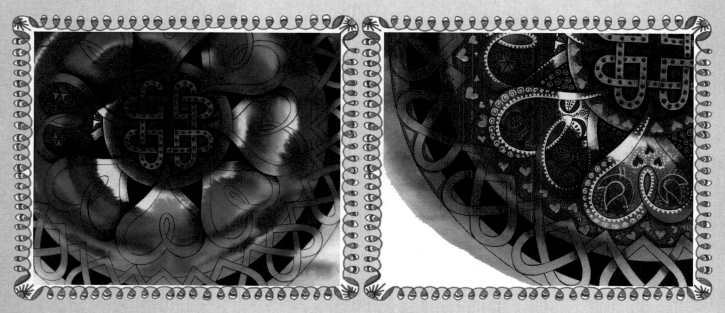

Use black ball-point hatching to make the middle band of hearts appear to tilt sideways. Fill in the dark areas of the composition.

Doodle alternate patterns of apples, maple leaves, roses, and turtle doves. Areas of white gel-pen doodles will add dramatic contrast.

Inspiration...

Use this finished artwork (above) as inspiration for your own
love & passion mandala. The outline of the design is printed
on the opposite page. It is ready for you to adapt, doodle, and
embellish however you wish!

Chapter Five

Sun & Moon Mandala

The Sun is an ancient symbol for the soul that lies deep within us. It carries with it masculine qualities such as inner drive, concentration, and ambition. Conversely, the Moon follows a monthly cycle of waxing and waning until it disappears, only to be reborn. The Moon has feminine qualities, including creativity and intuition; it appears to look outward where it finds comfort and inspiration.

The design at the center of this mandala is half-Sun, half-Moon to represent the unity of opposites: day and night, light and dark, male and female.

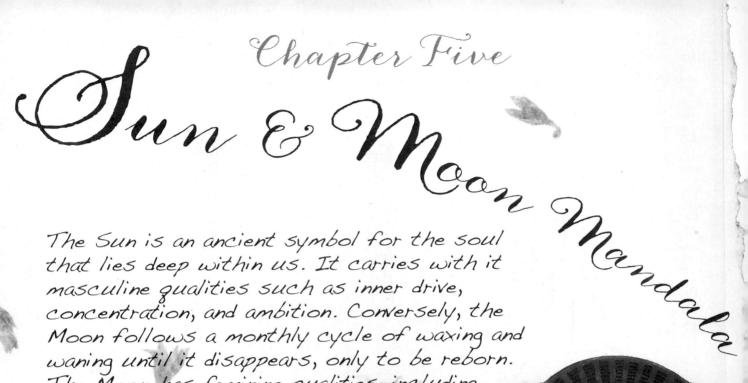

49

Central image

A strong central image is vital if you wish to focus the design on the center of the mandala. Don't rush the process of designing—make several rough sketches and thumbnails until you feel confident with your result.

Moonlight...

The black and white central motif stands out dramatically against the rest of the full-color doodles.

Half-Sun and half-Moon...

Color rough...

Make a color rough (or series of roughs) of your composition.
Contemplate the changes wrought by the Sun as it rises at dawn,
bringing light and warmth to the world. The sunflower heads that
follow the Sun as it traverses the sky make a beautiful repeating
pattern. Try to incorporate the Sun hiding behind clouds then shining
brightly after a sudden rainstorm.

Chapter Six
Earth & Water

Fragile

The Earth is our home. By protecting and providing for us, it gives us life. It is unbelievably complex, astoundingly beautiful, and also frighteningly fragile. Seven tenths of the Earth's surface is covered with water: the vital source of life for all living things. Even as water flows softly and gently, it is slowly and inexorably carving out its path through the solid rock face of our planet's surface.

57

The Tree of Life

...and mother nature

The Tree of Life is a very powerful image that symbolizes wisdom, protection, strength, abundance, beauty, and regeneration. This mandala combines the Tree of Life symbol with that of two strong hands to represent mother nature cradling the Earth.

Different designs

Hands around the world!

Try out different designs to see which works best. In this rough, the hands hold the Earth protectively. The hands in the drawing turn into two entwined trees to represent the Tree of Life.

Make thumbnail sketches
of your design.

Now work on your color rough.
Try to include water in its many
forms: tranquil lakes, crashing waves,
raindrop patterns, and falling snow.

Add the symbols
for Earth, Water,
Fire, and Air!

Earth

Air

Water

Fire

Reflections

Draw out your finished design. Think how water impacts on the Earth as you doodle into the artwork.

The reflections of landscapes in lakes and rivers make an effective starting point for doodling. This design also includes a bird, a beetle, a butterfly, a fox, a rabbit, a snake, a whale, and an octopus. These creatures represent the incredible diversity and wonder of the natural world.

Block in areas of flat color, always working outward from the center. Think of how the tonal value of each section relates to adjacent colors.

The curling tree-root shapes are echoed by the octopus's curling arms.

Try basing an area of doodles on the interesting patterns made by water ripples.

Color the leaves on the tree yellow. Add layers of different shades of green doodling to give depth and richness.

Inspiration!

The countless blues of the sea!

61

Inspiration...

Use the finished artwork (above) as inspiration for your own
Earth & water mandala. The outline of the design is printed on the
opposite page. It is ready for you to adapt, doodle, and embellish
however you wish!

63

Glossary

Analogous colors harmonious colors that are next to each other on the color diagram (see page 17).

Asymmetrical having parts that do not form a mirror image of one another across an axis.

Background the area behind and around the main object or image.

Celtic relating to an ancient culture located in the British Isles, Ireland, and parts of mainland Europe.

Colors of a rainbow red, orange, yellow, green, blue, indigo, and violet.

Complementary colors those that are opposite to each other on the color diagram (see page 17).

Composition how an artist arranges the different elements that make up a work of art.

Deconstruct to break down into basic components.

Enlightenment the attainment of spiritual knowledge or insight.

Graphic representation a vivid, clear, and effective depiction of an idea.

Hue the name of a color, irrespective of its lightness, darkness, or intensity.

Intensity a measurement of how different from pure gray a color is.

Layout arrangement, plan, or design.

Meditation stilling the mind, focusing it away from the everyday concerns of your verbal self, and listening inwardly.

Primary colors a trio of colors from which all other colors can be obtained by mixing.

Proportion the size, location, or amount of one part of an image in relation to another.

Rough a hasty, undetailed sketch of the main elements of a picture.

Secondary color a color that results from mixing two primary colors.

Shading the lines or marks used to fill in areas or represent gradations of color or darkness.

Sketch a quick, undetailed drawing.

Symbolism the representation of something in symbolic form.

Symmetrical consisting of similar parts facing each other in mirror image.

Technique the method used to produce something.

Tertiary color a color made by mixing one primary and one secondary color.

Thumbnail a very small, quick, abbreviated sketch.

Tonal value the lightness or darkness of part of an image, independent of its color or hue.